HEART
FOR
WOMEN

A 40-DAY DEVOTIONAL OF COMFORT, HOPE AND HEALING FOR WOMEN BREAKING FREE OF THE SHACKLES OF DOMESTIC VIOLENCE

MEREDITH SWIFT

© 2019 Meredith Swift

All rights reserved. No part of this publication may be reproduced, stored in a retrieval system or transmitted in any form or by any means electronic, mechanical, photocopying, recording or otherwise without prior written permission of the publisher. Short extracts may be used for review purposes.

Created in the Commonwealth of Australia.

All Scriptures are taken from the New Spirit-Filled Life Bible (© 2002), The Holy Bible, New King James version, © 1982 by Thomas Nelson, Inc. Used by permission. All rights reserved.

Cover Design by germancreative@Fiverr
Formatted by Jen Henderson @Wild Words Formatting

ISBN: 978-0-6485073-2-1

DEDICATION

This book is dedicated to my precious daughters, Sarah and Melissa, who are my beauty for ashes and my oil of joy for mourning.

This book is dedicated to all the women who have found the bravery and the courage to rise up from the depths of despair and break out of the prison of abuse; who dare to believe that there is a place of peace and of true refuge and rest, where they can be who God created them to be; who realise, with a faint and miniscule stirring—but just enough to spearhead the change—that God seeks the very best for us! God has a wonderful plan for each of our lives; for our good and for His glory! He invites us to bathe in His perfect love, through the One who is our true refuge and rest—Jesus! God promises that He will be our shield and our protection; our refuge and strength, a very present help in trouble (Psalm 46:1).

Aaronic Blessing: Numbers 6:24
The Lord bless you and keep you
25 The Lord make His face shine upon you
And be gracious to you
26 The Lord lift up His countenance upon you,
And give you peace.

John 3:16
For God so loved the world that He gave His only begotten Son, that whoever believes in Him should not perish but have everlasting life.

Isaiah 61:1

"The Spirit of the Lord GOD is upon Me;
Because the LORD has anointed Me
To preach good tidings to the poor;
He has sent Me to heal the broken hearted,
To proclaim liberty to the captives,
And the opening of the prison to those who are bound.
2 To proclaim the acceptable year of the LORD,
And the day of vengeance of our God,
To comfort all who mourn,
3 To console those who mourn in Zion,
To give beauty for ashes,
The oil of joy for mourning,
The garment of praise for the spirit of heaviness;
That they may be called trees of righteousness,
The planting of the LORD, that He may be glorified."

THANK YOU FOR READING MY BOOK!

You can visit my website and read my blog at:
https://www.meredithswift.org

PLEASE LEAVE A REVIEW

I really appreciate all of your feedback, and I love hearing what you have to say.

I need your input to make my future books better. Please leave me a helpful review on Amazon letting me know what you thought of the book. Each review is worth its weight in gold. I would be so grateful if you could do this!

TABLE OF CONTENTS

INTRODUCTION 1

DAY 1 – A COCOON OF FEAR 3

DAY 2 – FAR FROM YOUR MIND 5

DAY 3 – NOTHING IS WASTED 7

DAY 4 – BURDEN BEARER 9

DAY 5 – COMMUNING WITH ME 11

DAY 6 – I AM YOUR FOUNDATION 14

DAY 7 – SAFE HARBOUR 16

DAY 8 – PERIL IN THE ENOUGH! 18

DAY 9 – BREAKING FREE 20

DAY 10 – INHABITING SHAME 22

DAY 11 – CLEANSING TEARS 24

DAY 12 – NO MISTAKES 26

DAY 13 – POOLS OF WATER IN THE DESERT 28

DAY 14 – CHOOSING FORGIVENESS 30

DAY 15 – RESTORING YOU BACK 33

DAY 16 – OPENING TO RECEIVE 35

DAY 17 – ESSENTIAL TEARS 37

DAY 18 – RELINQUISHING FEARS 39

DAY 19 – BEAUTY FOR ASHES 41

DAY 20 – BINDING UP YOUR WOUNDS 43

DAY 21 – I AM WHO I SAY I AM 45

DAY 22 – BE WILLING TO HEAL 47

DAY 23 – PRECIOUS PROMISES 50

DAY 24 – SOOTHING HARSHNESS 52

DAY 25 – SEARCHING FOR INTIMACY 53

DAY 26 – SETTING BOUNDARIES 55

DAY 27 – DISSOLVING BARRIERS 57

DAY 28 – VENGEANCE IS MINE 59

DAY 29 – LOOSEN YOUR VOICE 62

DAY 30 – RETURN TO ME 64

DAY 31 – CAREFUL PREPARATION 66

DAY 32 – SWEET REFRESHING 69

DAY 33 – PLANTED IN MY GROUND 72

DAY 34 – LIFT YOUR HEAD 74

DAY 35 – LEAPING WITH JOY! 76

DAY 36 – TWO BECOME ONE 78

DAY 37 – MY THOROUGH WAYS 80

DAY 38 – THE MIGHT OF MY EMBRACE 82

DAY 39 – DAILY IMMERSION 84

DAY 40 – A NEW LIFE WAITING 86

CONCLUSION 89

RESOURCES 95

MY BOOKS 97

ACKNOWLEDGEMENTS AND THANKS 99

INTRODUCTION

Leaving my marriage permanently would have to be one of the hardest journeys I have ever undertaken. It was an intensely painful process to come to the realisation that the happily ever after I yearned for was never going to eventuate. My marriage was a battle zone for 20 years as I fled from and reconciled with my husband at least half a dozen times. Each time I returned, the abuse also returned, and each time was harder for me to bear. The utter desolation and entrapment of being in an abusive marriage can be soul destroying. I write about the journey of my marriage as part of my second book *"From New Age to New Creation – Set Free"* (available at https://www.amazon.com/dp/B07L7JV151).

When I left my husband for what turned out to be the final time and fled with my children to yet another refuge, I was overwhelmed with mixed emotions. I felt guilt and shame mixed with enormous relief that I was free of the abuse. I felt angry and resentful that my marriage had ended so harshly. In many ways I felt like a failure, with a heart that was raw and bloodied from the pain of my abusive marriage. I searched in desperation for Scriptures that would validate my decision to leave and reassure me that I was not being disobedient to God. Deep within myself I believed I had violated the covenant of my marriage and my belief was backed up by **Malachi 2:14**—God hates divorce.

This devotional is the one I wanted to read when I was in that refuge for the final time. It is a devotional to encourage and uplift the hurting heart of any woman who, like me, was overwhelmed by pain and drowning in sorrow and regret, guilt and grief, shame, doubt and fear. I often felt as though I was literally clinging to the hem of Jesus as He spoke words of comfort to soothe and heal the pain of what I was going through. Our precious Saviour Jesus is One well acquainted with suffering and persecution and His tenderness, His mercy, His love and His justice all helped my heart to heal. He became my heavenly husband (***Isaiah 54:5***), protective and providing, caring for and ministering to me.

I have chosen to make this a 40-day devotional because throughout the Bible, 40 is a number which emphasizes a time of trouble and hardship, followed by breakthrough and blessing. For example, we find this when Jesus spends 40 days in the wilderness (the trouble and hardship) before He begins His ministry (***Matthew 4:1-17***) (the breakthrough) and then spends another 40 days between His resurrection and ascension (***Acts 1:3***) (the blessing). Another example is where the Israelites spend 40 years in the wilderness (***Numbers 14:33-34*** and ***Deuteronomy 8:2-5***) (the trouble and hardship) before they are delivered into the Promised Land (the breakthrough and blessing).

It is my hope this devotional will help to lead you out of a time of trouble and hardship into breakthrough and blessing. For me, the biggest blessing has already been given to me the day I accepted Jesus Christ as my Lord and Saviour. At the Holy Cross of Jesus, our precious Saviour willingly gave His life so we could be forgiven of all our sins and never again be separated from our Heavenly Father God. The Cross is the place of forgiveness and signifies the means whereby those who come to Jesus are given the freedom of living in eternal relationship with Him. It is this freedom, forged within the unfathomable sacrifice of God's own Son dying for us, which is the overarching and underscoring theme of all that is contained within this devotional.

I invite you now to journey with me into God's heart for women and allow Him to reveal your sweet beauty and your unique worth to you; allow Him to permeate you at the deepest level with His immeasurable love and His utter delight in you; allow Him to fill you with His grace-drenched forgiveness and allow Him to be glorified as you step into His good, good plan for your life.

DAY 1 – A COCOON OF FEAR

Dearest child—

The comfort that you crave so desperately is available to you right here and right now. You are in a cocoon of fear, yet this cocoon will break open and you will be freed from it soon enough. This cocoon of fear seeks to *confine* you, but it cannot *define* you. In Me, you are so much more than this fear.

Rest now in My love, My transforming love, and know that I hold you close to Me, safe within My heart. Seek not to regret nor renounce the fears. Simply give them to Me and acknowledge that they do not serve you any longer. Rest in Me and together we will reclaim all those parts of your identity which are hidden and ashamed. Circumstances you found yourself within and decisions made were all built on the knowledge that you held at that time.

My precious child, I love and care for you. Allow Me to tenderly apply balm to your wounds of grief with My love and allow them to heal with My precious blood shed and with the drenching of My lifegiving Living Water.

Forgive as you have been forgiven and recognise that I am here always to assist you and to love you beyond measure.

Rest in Me.

MEREDITH SWIFT

Psalm 34:4

I sought the LORD, and He heard me,
And delivered me from all my fears.
5 They looked to Him and were radiant,
And their faces were not ashamed.

1 John 4:18

There is no fear in love; but perfect love casts out fear, because fear involves torment. But he who fears has not been made perfect in love. 19 We love Him because He first loved us.

DAY 2 – FAR FROM YOUR MIND

Precious child of Mine—

The hurt you have felt in the past is over and done with. Remove it far from your mind as you bring it to My Holy Cross. Allow the streams of My Living Water to wash away the accumulated memories and to flow through your body, heart, soul, spirit and mind—giving you new strength, new hope, new courage, new inspiration and new help. Let all of you be constantly renewed in this way.

As your Creator, I have infinite and varied ways in which to serve you and each day I recreate you anew—if you will allow this. It was I who fashioned you into being. It was I who created each and every part and all of you. Allow Me to continue to receive and hold every part of you by giving yourself to Me daily.

Renew each day with a fresh sense of purpose that you will live as I have intended. Follow Me.

Psalm 139:14
I will praise You, for I am fearfully and wonderfully made;
Marvellous are Your works,
And that my soul knows very well.

Isaiah 43:18
Do not remember the former things,
Nor consider the things of old.
19 Behold, I will do a new thing,
Now it shall spring forth;

Shall you not know it?
I will even make a road in the wilderness
And rivers in the desert.

Ephesians 4:20
But you have not so learned Christ, 21 if indeed you have heard Him and have been taught by Him, as the truth is in Jesus: 22 that you put off, concerning your former conduct, the old man which grows corrupt according to the deceitful lusts, 23 and be renewed in the spirit of your mind, 24 and that you put on the new man which was created according to God, in true righteousness and holiness.

DAY 3 – NOTHING IS WASTED

Beloved daughter—

All you have witnessed, all that you have taken into your being, all that you have suffered, the blows life has dealt you in the spiritual, mental, emotional and physical realms—all of these can be brought back unto Me for My glory and your good. Nothing is wasted. Believe Me when I say this. I teach what you need to learn. Nothing is wasted.

Come unto Me and give Me all that you have suffered. It is part of the fruit of the Spirit that this time of suffering develops patience within you. But you do not let it define you—rather, you allow Me to use it to refine the gold that I wish to cultivate within you.

As I gave My life willingly on that Cross I suffered long. At any given moment I could have stepped down off that Cross, yet I chose to die; to take on all the sins of the world, so that you could be truly and eternally free within Me. My arms were outstretched in My suffering as I took on all of your sin. My arms are still outstretched towards you. Choose to run into My embrace and allow Me to continue to take on all of your suffering, upholding and protecting you with My mighty strength and shielding you with My tender and loving sacrificial protection.

Praise Me! The Lord your God has delivered you.

Come to Me.

MEREDITH SWIFT

Isaiah 41:10
Fear not, for I am with you;
Be not dismayed, for I am your God,
I will strengthen you,
Yes, I will help you,
I will uphold you with My righteous
Right hand.

Psalm 28:7
The LORD is my strength and my
Shield;
My heart trusted in Him, and I am
Helped;
Therefore my heart greatly rejoices,
And with my song I will praise Him.

1 Peter 5:6
Therefore humble yourselves under the mighty hand of God, that He may exalt you in due time, 7 casting all your care upon Him, for He cares for you.

DAY 4 – BURDEN BEARER

Cherished daughter—

Meditate on all that is good, pure and lovely. Soak in My Word; meditate on My Word and repeat My Word until it permeates all of your being and is as natural to you as breathing in and out. And allow not the ugliness that has been perpetrated on you to guide you any longer. Yet come to Me and I will take all your burdens from you. I am the Burden bearer, the Healer of broken hearts, the Overcoming, the Almighty, All Powerful Lord of all creation!

Remember this when you are tempted to slide backwards and be lost within past events that threaten to strangle and thwart what we are rebuilding now. The healing comes when you give *all* to Me. I am your safety, your security, your All in All, your Saviour who hung on a Cross because of My unending love for you.

I, the spotless and defenceless lamb of God at that time, now protects and defends you and intercedes mightily for you. You need to know that nothing can separate us. Nothing can snatch you from Me if you choose to stay close to Me, encircled in My tender embrace and fierce protection. Choose what is real now. I am the way, the truth and the life and I have come to give you life and life abundantly.

My sweet and cherished daughter! You are so loved!

Rest in Me.

MEREDITH SWIFT

Isaiah 42:3

A bruised reed He will not break;
And smoking flax He will not quench;
He will bring forth justice for truth.

Matthew 11:28

"Come to Me, all you who labour and are heavy laden, and I will give you rest. 29 "Take My yoke upon you and learn from Me, for I am gentle and lowly in heart, and you will find rest for your souls. 30 "For My yoke is easy and My burden is light."

Romans 8:38

For I am persuaded that neither death nor life, nor angels nor principalities nor powers, nor things present nor things to come, 39 nor height nor depth, nor any other created thing, shall be able to separate us from the love of God which is in Christ Jesus our Lord.

John 10:10

The thief does not come except to steal, and to kill, and to destroy. I have come that they may have life, and that they may have it more abundantly.

DAY 5 – COMMUNING WITH ME

Precious daughter—

Let your "No" be "No" and your "Yes" be "Yes". Strengthen your inner man with fortitude found in the consistency of communing with Me; make captive any thought that is of your old way of pattern. You are a new creation in Me, and you are to recognise that your old thought patterns will emerge which will test this truth. Breaking bondages and strongholds is accomplished by giving them to Me; by praying unceasingly and giving thanks that you have new life within Me; by allowing trusted brothers and sisters in Christ to minister to you that you are worthy and that God has created you perfectly.

You are not damaged goods! You are My beautiful child, broken and believing of the lies of the enemy, yet made whole and blameless in My sight. I see you as My cherished possession; a shining and perfect pearl that irritation and pressure has formed; a sparkling jewel which shines with fire; gold that is purified and refined in the furnace of My unending and unfailing love and gentleness and mercy.

Come to Me now, My sweet and irreplaceable one, fearfully and wonderfully made in My image, and live in My promises of who you are. Your identity is in Me; yet this is a perilous time as you flip flop between this truth and the lies of the enemy. Keep your eyes on Me; allow Me to be the Lord of your life. For there is nothing you can give Me that I am not equipped to handle. I will show you who you are and Whose you are. For you belong to Me!

You are to take up your Cross of condemnation and carry it; give to Me all aspects of your life. This is a moment by moment choice that you can make, knowing that I will receive and transform what has been crushed and stolen from you.

Rest in My promises; for I am your Lord of restoration and restitution; I am your Jesus who hung on that Cross so that you may be set free from all that could separate us. So that you, in this fallen world, could come back to Me and be encircled in My shepherd love and fierce protectiveness. I came in search of you precious daughter and you are no longer lost and seeking.

Rest now in My overcoming and redeeming love. Remember—It is finished!

2 Corinthians 1:20
For all the promises of God in Him are Yes, and in Him Amen, to the glory of God through us. 21 Now He who establishes us with you in Christ and has anointed us is God, 22 who also has sealed us and given us the Spirit in our hearts as a guarantee.

Matthew 5:37
"But let your 'Yes' be 'Yes', and your 'No', 'No'. For whatever is more than these is from the evil one.

1 Peter 1:3
Blessed be the God and Father of our Lord Jesus Christ, who according to His abundant mercy has begotten us again to a living hope through the resurrection of Jesus Christ from the dead, 4 to an inheritance incorruptible and undefiled and that does not fade away, reserved in heaven for you, 5 who are kept by the power of God through faith for salvation ready to be revealed in the last time. 6 In this you greatly rejoice, though now for a little while, if need be, you have been grieved by various trials, 7 that the genuineness of your faith, being much more precious than gold that perishes,

though it is tested by fire, may be found to praise, honour, and glory at the revelation of Jesus Christ, 8 whom having not seen you love. Though now you do not see Him, yet believing, you rejoice with joy inexpressible and full of glory, receiving the end of your faith—the salvation of your souls.

Isaiah 48:10

Behold, I have refined you, but not as silver;
I have tested you in the furnace of affliction.

DAY 6 – I AM YOUR FOUNDATION

Sweet and anointed daughter—

Practice gentleness and patience as you become who I called you to be. Conform yourself only to the image of the Christ and not to the ways of this world, not to man. You are woman, helper to man, created from man yet still made in His image, in the image of God. Fashioned after His likeness and very good. Yet you are enslaved to a life where there is pain through childbirth, where your desire is to seek your husband first, rather than Me, and to instead crave *his* value and security as your foundation—rather than Mine. In this way, you are ruled by your husband and the right relationship with God as your focus becomes twisted. This is the curse from those far off times in that beautiful and perfect garden, fashioned and blessed by your loving, all-knowing and all-powerful God.

Yet at My Cross you are redeemed by Me, your Lord Jesus Christ, re-made in My image, chosen and set apart. You rise to become part of My holy priesthood. You are more than a conqueror within Me.

Woman. Beloved woman.

> ***Genesis 1:27***
> *So God created man in His own image; in the image of God He created him; male and female He created them.*

> ***Genesis 2:18***
> *And the LORD God said, "It is not good that man should be alone; I will make him a helper comparable to him."*

HEART FOR WOMEN

Romans 8:20-21

For the creation was subjected to futility, not willingly, but because of Him who subjected it in hope; 21 because the creation itself also will be delivered from the bondage of corruption into the glorious liberty of the children of God.

Romans 8:37

Yet in all these things we are more than conquerors through Him who loved us.

Romans 12:2

And do not be conformed to this world, but be transformed by the renewing of your mind, that you may prove what is that good and acceptable and perfect will of God.

1 Peter 2:9

But you are a chosen generation, a royal priesthood, a holy nation, His own special people, that you may proclaim the praises of Him who called you out of darkness into His marvellous light; 10 who once were not a people but are now the people of God, who had not obtained mercy but have now obtained mercy.

DAY 7 – SAFE HARBOUR

Precious most cherished daughter of Mine—

Every blow that rained down on your flesh and every evil word that was seared into your mind was a lie from the pit of Hell, sent to veil from your eyes the truth that you are a daughter of the Most High King. You are royalty. You were never created to be controlled—your free will and your ability to choose are an intrinsic part of who I have fashioned you to be. Within the boundaries of godly marriage, you are to be protected and provided for by your husband.

His strong arms and godly leadership are to be a safe harbour where you are free to be who I have created you to be—a woman of God, growing in maturity in Me, a godly mother who is the nurturer of your husband and children, who is the heart of your home and the protector of the heart of your husband. And the heart I have put into him is a heart which yearns to provide for you and is joyfully responsible for his family. Anything less than this is not of My design. There is no part in My Holy Scriptures for the domination of you, precious woman, for that is an ungodly and hollow vessel built on deceit. It is most certainly not of Me.

Rest safely now My daughter for you are free now to choose to live within My design of you. This journey will require courage now to allow for My gentle transformation. Your willingness is essential as I prune and cut back those parts of you that are no longer necessary in your walk with Me. This is an essential part of your growth and not to be rushed. Listen for My voice and lift your heart of obedience towards Me as I cleanse and restore that which has been tarnished and taken from you.

HEART FOR WOMEN

Be still and know that I am God.

Abide with Me.

1 Timothy 5:8
But if anyone does not provide for his own, and especially for those of his household, he has denied the faith and is worse than an unbeliever.

1 Peter 3:17
Husbands, likewise, dwell with them with understanding, giving honour to the wife, as to the weaker vessel, and as being heirs together of the grace of life, that your prayers may not be hindered.

Colossians 3:18
Wives, submit to your own husbands, as is fitting in the Lord. 19 Husbands, love your wives and do not be bitter toward them.

John 15:1
"I am the true vine, and My Father is the vinedresser. 2 "Every branch in Me that does not bear fruit He takes away; and every branch that bears fruit He prunes, that it may bear more fruit. 3 "You are already clean because of the word which I have spoken to you. 4 "Abide in Me, and I in you. As the branch cannot bear fruit of itself, unless it abides in the vine, neither can you, unless you abide in Me."

DAY 8 – PERIL IN THE ENOUGH!

Precious overcoming daughter—

Nothing is wasted. Every stitch in the fabric of your life is a stitch that is precious in My sight and able to be redeemed. Wounds can heal and words may be forgotten but My redeeming grace is such that these iniquities can be transcended. That sweet revelation of My grace is waiting. It is always there. We come to a point where there is no other choice but to say "Enough!". There is peril in the "Enough". It may seem that the "Enough" invokes greater harm but there is no power in this world that can stand against My transcending might!

Psalm 147:5

Great is our Lord, and mighty in power;
His understanding is infinite.

Isaiah 40:28

Have you not known? Have you not heard? The everlasting God, the LORD, The Creator of the ends of the earth, neither faints nor is weary. His understanding is unsearchable. 29 He gives power to the weak, and to those who have no might He increases strength. 30 Even the youths shall faint and be weary, And the young men shall utterly fall, 31 But those who wait on the LORD shall renew their strength; They shall mount up with wings like eagles, they shall run and not be weary, they shall walk and not faint.

HEART FOR WOMEN

1 Corinthians 6:14
And God both raised up the Lord and will also raise us up by His power.

Colossians 1:11
strengthened with all might, according to His glorious power, for all patience and longsuffering with joy; 12 giving thanks to the Father who has qualified us to be partakers of the inheritance of the saints in the light. 13 He has delivered us from the power of darkness and conveyed us into the kingdom of the Son of His love, 14 in whom we have redemption through His blood, the forgiveness of sins.

DAY 9 – BREAKING FREE

Precious jewel in My Crown—

I cherish you and I free you from the entrapment of your past. Come unto Me and give to Me that which wounds you at your core. You believe you are not enough; you wish you were more. You are crippled by the belief that you are falling short. Yet I have come to free you from the bondage that keeps you trapped and paralysed. For as a spider cocoons its prey you are held tight and fast by the bondage of the enemy.

Your suffering and torment lay claim to you because you exist in a state where you believe that at some point in the future all will be different and made right. I say to you, when you give your life to Me, you are instantly made right in My eyes. Here and now, all your sins are forgiven. You need not suffer the lie that you are not enough. Give yourself to Me and believe Me when I say to you that you are forgiven. You are enough, precious child. You are loved! You are cherished!

You are Mine!

> *Ephesians 2:10*
> *For we are His workmanship, created in Christ Jesus for good works, which God prepared beforehand that we should walk in them.*

> *2 Corinthians 3:17*
> *Now the Lord is the Spirit; and where the Spirit of the Lord is, there is liberty. 18 But we all, with unveiled face, beholding as in a mirror the glory of the Lord, are being transformed into the same image from glory to glory, just as by the Spirit of the Lord.*

HEART FOR WOMEN

John 8:36

"Therefore, if the Son makes you free, you shall be free indeed."

Isaiah 53:3

He is despised and rejected by men, A Man of sorrows and acquainted with grief. And we hid, as it were, our faces from Him. He was despised, and we did not esteem Him. 4 Surely He has borne our griefs and carried our sorrows; Yet we esteemed Him stricken, smitten by God, and afflicted. 5 But He was wounded for our transgressions, He was bruised for our iniquities, The chastisement for our peace was upon Him, And by His stripes we are healed.

DAY 10 – INHABITING SHAME

My broken and beautiful one—

The shame that inhabits you also covers you. You seek to hide yourself away, to define yourself as not just lacking but as lack itself. As though your existence makes no difference to anyone in this world. As though the plan I have for your life is not good. As though you being alive is of no consequence for My glory. As though you are less than nothing.

Bound hand and foot, paralysed with an inability to rise above your circumstances and when you do rise above them, to be dragged back into the mire of doubt and wondering and wishing that things were different. Can you be perfect? No, you cannot. Yet I, your perfect Creator, am perfection itself. And I, your Creator, can lift you above any circumstance you may find yourself in. Choose not to surrender to the lies the enemy whispers into your soul but rather to surrender to Me— your Almighty, loving, merciful, just God, who has all the moments of your life firmly in My hand.

All that I require is you. The you I created, the you who I fashioned so lovingly and fearfully and wonderfully. You are unique. I require the you who trusts and seeks to obey My Sovereign Word, to lean in close to Me and cling to Me. You can do all things through He who strengthens you.

> *Philippians 4:12*
> *I know how to be abased, and I know how to abound. Everywhere and in all things I have learned both to be full and to be hungry, both to abound and to suffer need. 13 I can do all things through Christ who strengthens me.*

HEART FOR WOMEN

Psalm 26:3

For Your lovingkindness is before my eyes, And I have walked in Your truth.

Hebrews 12:2

Looking unto Jesus, the author and finisher of our faith, who for the joy that was set before Him endured the Cross, despising the shame, and has sat down at the right hand of the throne of God.

DAY 11 – CLEANSING TEARS

Precious child—

Cry your tears, for they cleanse the darkness that is hidden within your soul. Cleansing tears create within you the clean heart that I desire. Vulnerability breaks open the shell of control and you are then able to come forth in rawness and weakness. This is what I require—for in your weakness I am made strong.

I use that weakness so that you may learn to rely on Me, because you are My fragile creation, and much loved in your frailty and humanness. For I am your God, your majestic God, Creator of all that is. You are My beloved creation, made in My image. Allow Me to be your Protector and you will be an overcomer in Me. Realise that you can do nothing apart from nor separate from My eternal love, My eternal might and My eternal steadfastness.

Abide with Me.

Psalm 51:10
Create in me a clean heart, O God,
And renew a steadfast spirit within me.

Psalm 126:5
Those who sow in tears shall reap in joy. 6 He who continually goes forth weeping, bearing seed for sowing, shall doubtless come again with rejoicing, bringing his sheaves with him.

HEART FOR WOMEN

2 Corinthians 12:9

And He said to me, "My grace is sufficient for you, for My strength is made perfect in weakness." Therefore, most gladly I will rather boast in my infirmities, that the power of Christ may rest upon me.

John 11:35

Jesus wept.

DAY 12 – NO MISTAKES

Beloved daughter of Mine—

The apple of My eye; My cherished creation!

Do not regret the past, for it has helped you to remember who you are and Whose you are. The hardship of your past was necessary in some measure for the shaping of your character. The darkness of those times would in times to come be the foundation for the light to shine. The light would reveal the darkness within you that had been forged by the lies of the enemy.

For I am the Light of the World. My plan is redemptive, transforming and complete. There are no mistakes, precious child of Mine. And just as you cannot see the panorama of a landscape unless you are sitting on a mountain top, so too could you never hope to see the panoramic masterpiece of your life when you were in the valleys of despair and desperation.

Yet the cry of your heart did not go unanswered. I am here now, as I was with you then—though you could not hope to see Me. Yet I was there, with My hand of protection on you and the wings of My angels wrapped around you to keep you safe and to preserve your life. **That life is so precious to Me!**

Remember, My child, you are here to make a difference. Remember I have set you free. Your pain can no longer define you. Your past is dissolved - so cast it far from you, just as I have cast your sin far from Me. Abide now in My peace and within My joy. I love you always and have done so since the beginning. There now is no end to My love for you. Peace be with you.

HEART FOR WOMEN

Romans 5:1

Therefore, having been justified by faith, we have peace with God through our Lord Jesus Christ, 2 through whom also we have access by faith into this grace in which we stand, and rejoice in hope of the glory of God. 3 And not only that, but we also glory in tribulations, knowing that tribulation produces perseverance; 4 and perseverance, character; and character, hope. 5 Now hope does not disappoint, because the love of God has been poured out in our hearts by the Holy Spirit who was given to us.

Ephesians 5:8

For you were once darkness, but now you are light in the Lord. Walk as children of light 9 (for the fruit of the Spirit is in all goodness, righteousness, and truth), 10 finding out what is acceptable to the Lord. 11 And have no fellowship with the unfruitful works of darkness, but rather expose them.

Psalm 91:11

For He shall give His angels charge over you, To keep you in all your ways.

DAY 13 – POOLS OF WATER IN THE DESERT

Beloved daughter—

You have been wandering in the desert with parched mouth and dry heart, devoid of love and starving from lack of dignity and worth. Yet I your Lord God, your Creator, create pools of water in the desert and living springs from that which has been completely dry. You had believed that your journeying was aimless, yet your wandering heart always had a destination. You were able to push through and overcome for I was there to carry you, to lift you up and shield you from the heat that would have melted you.

It would appear to you that you wished for an end to your existence. Yet I your Creator God - Who created you as unique and held your existence in the palm of My hand - did not decree then, nor do I decree now, that you would cease to exist as though your life was nothing.

Your life is as a speck of dust. From dust you come and to dust you return, but *you* are in no way as a speck of dust, insignificant and of no consequence. You are Mine and My plan for your life is good. You are out of the desert now, though in times to come as you journey on, your spirit will return to dryness. Know that My Living Water will be available to fill you up and refresh you. But this must come from your willingness to journey with Me.

For I am with you in your desert, in your lushness, in your dryness and in your overflowingness. I am with you at all times. But you must have eyes to see, ears to hear and a heart and mind that are willing to receive Me.

I love you My precious and anointed daughter. Always and forever.

HEART FOR WOMEN

Psalm 107:35

He turns a wilderness into pools of water, And dry land into water springs.

Mark 12:30

Jesus answered him, "The first of all the commandments is, 'Hear, O Israel, the LORD our God, the LORD is one. 30 'And you shall love the LORD your God with all your heart, with all your soul, with all your mind, and with all your strength.' This is the first commandment.'

John 4:14

"but whoever drinks of the water that I shall give him will never thirst. But the water that I shall give him will become in him a fountain of water springing up into everlasting life."

John 7:38

"He who believes in Me, as the Scripture has said, out of his heart will flow rivers of living water."

DAY 14 – CHOOSING FORGIVENESS

My cherished overcoming daughter—

The forgiveness that is essential in your walk is a choice. It stems from willingness. A willingness to step out of the prison of hardness and unyieldingness that keeps you caged. Your forgiveness has nothing to do with your appeared captor but everything to do with what you choose. Your ability to forgive is the difference between your heart being encased in cement and your heart being freed and softened, warm and vital, beating and pulsating with fresh new life.

You are no longer imprisoned by the lies that sought to engulf you, but now your choice will determine the texture and shape of your life as you journey forward. I have instructed in My Holy Scriptures to continually forgive; and this is because there are layers of forgiveness. The layers begin on the surface and go deeper and deeper. So, as you go deeper and deeper into the heart and the mind that I created within you, the need for forgiveness and your ability to forgive reveals itself further.

Allow the memories to come and as they emerge, bring them to My Holy Cross and give them to Me. Ask for My help in your forgiveness process. As it is a process. Allow your tears to cleanse and allow your heart to open. Ask Me to help you forgive. This process has everything to do with you and what you choose to do. It is your journey and it is your means towards true freedom. The lies of holding on cause your heart to harden. You have lived enough of that way. Yet My way is the way, the truth and the life and forgiveness is central to this.

For as I forgave you when I died for you, My precious and most beloved daughter, so too can you in turn forgive what life and circumstance and people have perpetrated upon you. Your salvation depended on My willingness to give My life for you; I willingly gave it. Your freedom from the sting and bondage of death depended on My willingness to forgive all your sin past present and future and cast it far from Me so that I remembered it no more. This was never easy, but I chose to do this.

Choose now to forgive and continue to choose this way. For it will truly set you free.

Peace be with you.

Matthew 5:43

"You have heard that it was said, 'You shall love your neighbour and hate your enemy.' 44 "But I say to you, love your enemies, bless those who curse you, do good to those who hate you, and pray for those who spitefully use you and persecute you, 45 'that you may be sons of your Father in heaven; for He makes His sun rise on the evil and on the good, and sends rain on the just and on the unjust.

Colossians 2:13

And you, being dead in your trespasses and the uncircumcision of your flesh, He has made alive together with Him, having forgiven you all trespasses, 14 having wiped out the handwriting of requirements that was against us, which was contrary to us. And He has taken it out of the way, having nailed it to the Cross. 15 Having disarmed principalities and powers, He made a public spectacle of them, triumphing over them in it.

Colossians 3:12

Therefore, as the elect of God, holy and beloved, put on tender mercies, kindness, humility, meekness, longsuffering; 13 bearing with one another, if anyone has a complaint against another, even as Christ forgave you, so you also must do.

Luke 6:36

"Therefore be merciful, just as your Father also is merciful. 37 "Judge not, and you shall not be judged. Condemn not, and you shall not be condemned. Forgive, and you will be forgiven. 38 "Give, and it will be given to you: good measure, pressed down, shaken together, and running over will be put into your bosom. For with the same measure that you use, it will be measured back to you."

Hebrews 12:17

For you know that afterward, when he wanted to inherit the blessing, he was rejected, for he found no place for repentance, though he sought it diligently with tears.

DAY 15 – RESTORING YOU BACK

Beloved daughter —

My precious jewel and My delight!

Grow strong in the promises I have for you. I restore you back into the original Plan I have for your life. Rest assured that My plan is good, for I seek My glorification from you. You have a purpose and I created you fearfully and wonderfully, beautifully and uniquely one of a kind. There is no-one else—no, none like you precious daughter of Mine.

Keep your eyes firmly fixed on Me and seek My ways. My unfailing love shall clothe you and protect you from any ravages. Only seek Me and you shall find Me. Seek earnestly and truly and I will be there. I go ahead and prepare the way yet here I am, right beside you. Rest in My promises, beloved child, and do not doubt that I am truth. For My love of you is unmatched. You are so loved!

Jeremiah 29:11
For I know the thoughts that I think towards you, says the LORD, thoughts of peace and not of evil, to give you a future and a hope.

Proverbs 3:5
Trust in the LORD with all your heart, And lean not on your own understanding; 6 In all your ways acknowledge Him, And He shall direct your paths.

1 Corinthians 13:13
And now abide faith, hope, love, these three; but the greatest of these is love.

Matthew 6:33

"But seek first the kingdom of God and His righteousness, and all these things shall be added to you. 34 "Therefore do not worry about tomorrow, for tomorrow will worry about its own things. Sufficient for the day is its own trouble."

DAY 16 – OPENING TO RECEIVE

Beloved child of Mine—

Cry out to Me in your desperation and in your pain! Cry out to Me when no words can come, when the weight and burden of your past would seem to crush you. Cry out to Me when you are frozen with fear and unable to move. Cry out to Me!

I hear you!

I will scoop you up in My loving embrace; I will tenderly bind up your wounds; I will soothe you and gently rock you as the loving Father that I am rocks His precious newborn baby. For you in many ways are like a newborn baby in this season of your life. Allow others to care for you; allow others to comfort you; allow others to give to you and allow yourself to receive.

This is not an easy thing when you have been so conditioned and used to receiving nothing. When the messages of hatred and deceit and worthlessness have wreaked havoc with your right to even be alive, much less your ability to receive. Yet your ability to receive is essential in this time of healing and restoration.

Receive wise counsel on your road to recovery.

Receive My love as I work through people, places, events and things to tend to your wounds and allow them to heal.

Receive the gift of life renewed.

For you are loved. You are worthy. You are Mine. My beloved daughter!

Peace be with you.

MEREDITH SWIFT

Psalm 23:1

The LORD is my shepherd; I shall not want. 2 He makes me to lie down in green pastures; He leads me beside the still waters. 3 He restores my soul; He leads me in the paths of righteousness For His name's sake. 4 Yea, though I walk through the valley of the shadow of death, I will fear no evil; For you are with me; Your rod and Your staff, they comfort me. 5 You prepare a table before me in the presence of my enemies; You anoint my head with oil; My cup runs over. 6 Surely goodness and mercy shall follow me All the days of my life; And I will dwell in the house of the LORD forever.

Matthew 7:7

"Ask, and it will be given to you; seek, and you will find, knock, and it will be opened to you. 8 "For everyone who asks receives, and he who seeks finds, and to him who knocks it will be opened."

John 14:13

"And whatever you ask in My name, that I will do, that the Father may be glorified in the Son. 14 "If you ask anything in My name, I will do it."

Philippians 4:6

Be anxious for nothing, but in everything by prayer and supplication, with thanksgiving, let your requests be known to God; and the peace of God, which surpasses all understanding, will guard your hearts and minds through Christ Jesus.

DAY 17 – ESSENTIAL TEARS

Beloved daughter—

Cry your tears, precious child. Cry your tears. For not one of them is wasted. All of them are restorative and cleansing.

Some may be tears of bitterness and desperation; some may be tears of relief and joy; others may be tears of sorrow so deep as to appear to be a bottomless pit that has no end. You may fear that once you begin to cry, you will never stop—like a dam that has burst its banks and spills out, flooding the land. Do not fear any of this, My precious child.

Your tears are absolutely necessary; absolutely essential as you heal and move into your future journey.

I collect every single one of your tears that are shed. And just as My Living Water fills you with power and might and love; so too will your cleansing tears, shed without censure, start to strip away and dissolve barriers of fear and distress; will begin to soothe memories of torment and brokenness. Each tear you shed allows for layers of hardness to be dissolved. Collectively, through your vulnerability and willingness to cry, your tears are a means by which you strengthen your spirit.

Cry your tears beloved child. Allow them!

Cry your tears.

Abide with Me.

MEREDITH SWIFT

Psalm 56:8

You number my wanderings, Put my tears into Your bottle; Are they not in Your book?

Luke 6:21

Blessed are you who hunger now, For you shall be filled. Blessed are you who weep now, For you shall laugh.

Revelation 21:4

And God will wipe away every tear from their eyes; there shall be no more death, nor sorrow, nor crying. There shall be no more pain, for the former things have passed away. 5 Then He who sat on the throne said, "Behold, I make all things new." And He said to me, "Write, for these words are true and faithful."

DAY 18 – RELINQUISHING FEARS

My precious daughter—

For I have not given you the spirit of fear, but of power and of love and of a sound mind.

The spirit of fear is NOT from Me; I have not given it to you. Yet I can take your fears from you, if you choose to give them to Me. I am your Creator and I transform fear to love. For My perfect love will cast out any of the fears which threaten to cripple you.

Allow yourself the courage of relinquishing fears to Me. For this does take courage. Fear has become such an integral part of who you believe yourself to be that you need courage to decide to start letting the fears go. You have allowed the fear to define you for long enough. You have lived in fear long enough; allowing it to take up residence within you. Fear does have a purpose as it alerts you to peril and can act as a barometer when a situation is not of Me. But I say to you: do not allow the fear—any fear—to become greater than your trust in Me.

Read My Scriptures, for they will be your armour of protection as you fill yourself with knowledge and knowing of Who I am and Whose you are. At every opportunity, speak with Me, listen for My still, small voice, pray to Me and repent of all that has kept you from Me. These practices will begin to strengthen you and your strengthening will increase as your fears dissolve.

You are forging a new identity, free from the fears which the enemy sought to paralyse you with. Take courage and step into this new beginning. Build a new foundation free from fear by trusting in Me, by growing your character within Me and above all, by allowing My precious blood to wash you clean, to purify you and bring you power.

Fear not, for I am with you to the end of days.

2 Timothy 1:7
For I have not given you the spirit of fear, but of power, and of love, and of a sound mind.

Isaiah 26:3
You will keep him in perfect peace, Whose mind is stayed on You, because he trusts in You. 4 Trust in the LORD forever, For in YAH, the Lord, is everlasting strength.

Jeremiah 17:7
Blessed is the man who trusts in the LORD, And whose hope is the LORD. 8 For he shall be like a tree planted by the waters, Which spreads out its roots by the river, And will not fear when heat comes; But its leaf will be green, And will not be anxious in the year of drought, Nor will cease from yielding fruit.

1 Kings 19:11
Then He said, "Go out, and stand on the mountain before the LORD." And behold, the LORD passed by, and a great and strong wind tore into the mountain and broke the rocks in pieces before the LORD, but the LORD was not in the wind; and after the wind an earthquake, but the LORD was not in the earthquake; 12 And after the earthquake a fire, but the LORD was not in the fire; and after the fire a still small voice.

DAY 19 – BEAUTY FOR ASHES

Precious child—

Your mother's heart regrets the violence your children witnessed. It tears at your heart and shatters your peace. This can be as an all-consuming fire—if you allow it to be. You cannot change your past! But know this, beloved daughter—I, only I, know the pieces of your life puzzle and how your story and the story of your children are entwined and interlocked with My story. I, only I, know how My good plan for your life and for theirs unfolds. I, only I, can know the ripple effect of the events of your life and of theirs and how I will be glorified through and in amongst all of these.

Your regret serves no purpose at this point in your life. Your guilt and your regret are as dust. Bring those things you regret and feel guilt about to My Holy Cross. Realise you are now at a different point in your journey and concentrate all of your actions with My love as your foundation. For the enemy comes to steal, kill and destroy. Do not allow him to steal your joy by regretting what was. Do not allow him to kill your hope by reliving what was. Nor to destroy the gift of freedom you have found because you now belong to Me.

Believe on Me and fill your mind and your heart with My promises and with My redemptive, overcoming, healing and mighty love. For I know you thoroughly and I can care for you completely. Only choose to come to Me. Only choose to abide with Me. Only choose to give all of your broken pieces to Me. And I will give you beauty for ashes. I will restore all that has been taken from you. For I am your redeeming and mighty God. I Am!

Peace be with you.

MEREDITH SWIFT

Proverbs 15:13
A merry heart makes a cheerful countenance, But by sorrow of the heart the spirit is broken.

1 John 1:9
If we confess our sins, He is faithful and just to forgive us our sins and to cleanse us from all unrighteousness.

1 Peter 5:10
But may the God of all grace, who called us to His eternal glory by Christ Jesus, after you have suffered a while, perfect, establish, strengthen, and settle you.

1 Corinthians 3:11
For no other foundation can anyone lay than that which is laid, which is Jesus Christ.

2 Timothy 2:19
Nevertheless the solid foundation of God stands, having this seal: "The Lord knows those who are His," and "Let everyone who names the name of Christ depart from iniquity."

DAY 20 – BINDING UP YOUR WOUNDS

Precious child—

Allow Me to minister to you. Allow Me to bind up your wounds with My tender loving care. Allow Me to love you by filling your mind and your heart with Me. Abide with Me. Seek My presence and I will fill you with My Living Water, I will quench the parched and arid landscape of your heart and mind with My Living Water. I will apply balm to your brokenness and pour out My precious and redemptive blood to wash away your harshness and soften your sorrows.

Let Me be with you. Chase after Me with your heart full of longing for Me and for My Holy word and I will turn and meet you at your deepest need. Take the steps toward Me and I will scoop you up in My tender and loving embrace, My sweet and merciful Father's arms. I am your lion of Judah, your stronghold in times of weakness, your watchtower of protection when you are fearful and feeling as though you are worth nothing. What you are worth to Me is something you cannot hope to comprehend. My love is all encompassing and all knowing.

Fear not, for I am your God.

I love you with a love that is unmatched in its majesty, which is unfathomable in its power, which is unknowable in its mystery.

Believe on Me!

MEREDITH SWIFT

1 Chronicles 10:11
Yours, O LORD, is the greatness, The power and the glory, The victory and the majesty; For all that is in heaven and in earth is Yours; Yours is the kingdom, O LORD, And You are exalted as head over all.

Psalm 147:3
He heals the broken hearted and binds up their wounds 4 He counts the number of the stars; He calls them all by name. 5 Great is our Lord, and mighty in power; His understanding is infinite.

Romans 5:5
Now hope does not disappoint, because the love of God has been poured out in our hearts by the Holy Spirit who was given to us. 6 For when we were still without strength, in due time Christ died for the ungodly. 7 For scarcely for a righteous man will one die; yet perhaps for a good man someone would even dare to die. 8 But God demonstrates His own love toward us, in that while were still sinners, Christ died for us.

Ephesians 5:2
And walk in love, as Christ also has loved us and given Himself for us, an offering and a sacrifice to God for a sweet-smelling aroma.

DAY 21 – I AM WHO I SAY I AM

Beloved daughter—

Praise and worship Me precious child! Sing praises to your most High God who has delivered you from evil. For in this My will has been done! Come to Me with your heart of thanksgiving and gratitude for what I have done for you. For what I *am* doing for you. For what I will continue to do as I shield you with My strong and mighty hand and the power of My Holy Spirit illuminating My Holy Scriptures. Come to Me and dance before Me, sing loudly and with intention to praise Me, your Creator God, your redeeming and merciful One, the One who set you free from the chains of death and the bondage of your sin.

And allow your praise and worship to Me strip away the layers of desperation, of pain, of terror, of hurt, of distress, of despair, of doubt and humiliation, of all that caused you to be trapped in the pit of lies and deceit which the enemy sought to strangle you with. Allow your praise and worship to fill you with a sweetness of spirit as you come into My presence, as you come before Me in My holy throne room. Allow your praise and worship to Me to shine light within your hidden darkness. Allow your praise and worship to Me to bring joy and sureness that I am Who I say I am—your merciful and loving Saviour, the Lord of all creation, who stepped down from glory and became a man so that our relationship could forever be restored.

Sing from your heart precious child, with abandon and intention all at once—to praise Me!

For I am your God.

I am your Lord Jesus Christ.

MEREDITH SWIFT

You are Mine and I am yours.

Peace be with you.

John 4:24
God is Spirit, and those who worship Him must worship in spirit and truth.

Psalm 86:9
All nations whom You have made shall come and worship before You, O Lord, And shall glorify Your name. 10 For You are great, and do wondrous things; You alone are God. 11 Teach me Your way, O LORD; I will walk in Your truth; Unite my heart to fear Your name. 12 I will praise You, O Lord my God, with all my heart, And I will glorify Your name forevermore.

Psalm 100:1
Make a joyful shout to the LORD, all you lands! 2 Serve the LORD with gladness, Come before His presence with singing. 3 Know that the LORD, He is God; It is He who has made us, and not we ourselves; We are His people and the sheep of His pasture. 4 Enter into His gates with thanksgiving, And into His courts with praise. Be thankful to Him, and bless His name. 5 For the LORD is good; His mercy is everlasting, And His truth endures to all generations.

Psalm 28:7
The LORD is my strength and my shield; My heart trusted in Him, and I am helped; Therefore my heart greatly rejoices, And with my song I will praise Him.

DAY 22 – BE WILLING TO HEAL

Beloved daughter—

My intention to raise up godly fathers and husbands is that these men of honour will protect, provide for, nurture and praise their wives. That their wives will be—as Eve was for Adam—a helper for them. That you, precious woman, as the weaker vessel should be lovingly cared for and protected at all costs. Your worth was never to be underestimated nor undermined. Anything less than this is not within My design. It is not from Me. For you are to be cherished. You are to be loved. You are to be honoured. You are to be nurtured. You are to be loved and known deeply. And you are to do likewise for your husband. For both of you together form the one and your bond shall be unbreakable and everlasting.

You who have known fear, control, manipulation, lack, powerlessness, deceit and terror at the hands of your husband can now relinquish these to Me. Know that they are the work of the enemy who is here on this fallen earth, roaring like a prowling lion, and that through My finished work at the Cross, you will learn to overcome all of these.

And overcome you shall, my precious child, through My might and power. Your weakness is made strong within Me.

Turn your face to Me now and be willing to heal. Through skilled intervention of wise counsellors, through places in nature, through discipline and consistency in routine, through play and joy and laughter and through obedience to Me and My Holy ways. All of these things can work together in order that you be healed from the wounds that have crippled you in past times. Your wounds will heal. Allow no bitterness, regret, guilt, shame or any other lie from the devil to cause those wounds to become infected. Allow for the healing to come. Believe this and do all that is necessary in order for this to be so. Allow gentleness to soothe your weary spirit.

For My plan for you is good. I will be glorified.

Rest now, precious child of Mine.

2 Corinthians 2:14
Now thanks be to God who always leads us in triumph in Christ, and through us diffuses the fragrance of His knowledge in every place.

Romans 16:20
And the God of peace will crush Satan under your feet shortly. The grace of our Lord Jesus Christ be with you. Amen.

1 John 5:4
For whatever is born of God overcomes the world. And this is the victory that has overcome the world—our faith.

Proverbs 31:10
Who can find a virtuous wife? For her worth is far above rubies. 11 The heart of her husband safely trusts her; So he will have no lack of gain.

Proverbs 31:28
Her children rise up and call her blessed; Her husband also, and he praises her.

HEART FOR WOMEN

1 Corinthians 11:11 Nevertheless, neither is man independent of woman, nor woman independent of man, in the Lord. 12 For as woman comes from man, even so man also comes through woman; but all things are from God.

DAY 23 – PRECIOUS PROMISES

Precious daughter of Mine—

I have loved you with infinite care and gentleness in all of your brokenness and I will continue to pour out My love and healing transformation as you journey within and through your pain at this time. The pain of separation and the destruction of your cherished dream that your marriage could have been good and growthful is raw and so close. You wonder at the purpose for all that you went through. Know this: your suffering is not wasted My dearest one. For I waste nothing. Know this: that I turn evil for good and I give you beauty for ashes.

I will redeem to you all of those lost years, all of those times of anguished suffering when you shrank in terror, tormented and belittled, lost in degradation and humiliation and paralysed by the relentless harshness of your ungodly union. When you believed that you did not want to exist one more moment in the painful prison that was your marriage.

I say to you that you can now know true freedom. Your freedom is in Me and in My overcoming love. I guide you to be an overcomer, precious daughter, an overcomer of all the lies of venom the enemy sought to plant within your mind. Those lies had grown into an overpowering jungle of noxious weeds but systematically they have been pulled out at the roots by My transforming promises of how I see you and who you are in Me. You belong to Me. My promises for you are good and solid.

The landscape of your mind is now to be filled with thoughts of Me. Let these precious promises made by Me become as flowers which bloom, imparting their sweet fragrance and soft petals to make your landscape beautiful in its colour and volume. I created you, precious woman of value, and I hold you in the palm of My Creator's hand. Nothing can prevail against the might and power of Who I Am.

Do not doubt who I see you to be. Let My unfailing love for you soak into you at the deepest core of your being; allow it to fill you and sustain you with the truth and the freedom that knowing Me brings.

Rest precious child and renew your spirit in Me.

For your story is not over.

Abide with Me.

1 Peter 1:3
Blessed be the God and Father of our Lord Jesus Christ, who according to His abundant mercy has begotten us again to a living hope through the resurrection of Jesus Christ from the dead, 4 to an inheritance incorruptible and undefiled and that does not fade away, reserved in heaven for you, 5 who are kept by the power of God through faith for salvation ready to be revealed in the last time. 6 In this you greatly rejoice, though now for a little while, if need be, you have been grieved by various trials, 7 that the genuineness of your faith, being much more precious than gold that perishes, though it is tested by fire, may be found to praise, honour, and glory at the revelation of Jesus Christ.

DAY 24 – SOOTHING HARSHNESS

Beloved daughter—

Cultivate gentleness for harshness; allow love to transform fear; exalt joy in exchange for sin; bring peace for chaos; recognise that your longsuffering has not been wasted yet will build your character; welcome kindness to soothe the harshness that was your portion; know that My plan for you is good and glorifying to Me; and know too that I am ever faithful. Bring self-control as you harness all those thoughts that are not from Me. All of the hatred and envy, the provocations, the jealousies and outbursts of wrath are not of My Kingdom. Walk in the Spirit, precious one, and allow the fruit of the Spirit to be cultivated within you.

You are Mine and I am yours.

Always and forever, even to the end of this age.

Peace be with you as you overcome in Me.

> *Proverbs 28:13*
> *He who covers his sins will not prosper, But whoever confesses and forsakes them will have mercy.*

> *Galatians 5:22*
> *But the fruit of the Spirit is love, joy, peace, longsuffering, kindness, goodness, faithfulness, gentleness, self-control. Against such there is no law. 24 And those who are Christ's have crucified the flesh with its passions and desires. 25 If we live in the Spirit, let us walk in the Spirit.*

DAY 25 – SEARCHING FOR INTIMACY

Precious daughter, beloved and cherished child of Mine—

The intimacy that you craved within your marriage was not available to you. You sought to become one with your husband and for the flesh of the two of you to cleave together. Instead you found division, separation, isolation and separation. You were cut off not only from your husband but from the eternality of My love, which is a nourishing and sustaining giver of life. There was danger in your quest for closeness as this was a threat to the domination that was sought by your spouse.

You can come to Me in safety and trust and with your search for intimacy. You can find it within the embrace of My unfailing love and within the whisperings of My Holy Spirit sent to guide and serve you, which speak wholeness and authenticity. My voice of truth speaks and pours intimacy into your innermost being. For intimacy is authenticity and I as your Creator am infallible in My authenticity. Dwell within Me and you cannot be moved, nor can you be shaken. I will never leave you nor forsake you, nor can I be anything but completely trustworthy.

You may develop absolute trust and find the joy that you seek as you commune with Me in safety and security. True intimacy is being known; being vulnerable and open and willing to be known. So when you come to Me in obedience with all that you are, all your doubts and fears, joys and sorrows, uncertainties, doubts and yearning for love, know that you are pleasing to Me and know that we are developing the deepest and most intimate of relationships. You as My created child and I as your Creator God.

MEREDITH SWIFT

Philippians 3:8

Yet indeed I also count all things loss for the excellence of the knowledge of Christ Jesus my Lord, for whom I have suffered the loss of all things, and count them as rubbish, that I may gain Christ 9 and be found in Him, not having my own righteousness, which is from the law, but that which is through faith in Christ, the righteousness which is from God by faith; 10 that I may know Him and the power of His resurrection and the fellowship of His sufferings, being conformed to His death.

Psalm 62:5

My soul, wait silently for God alone, For my expectation is from Him. 6 He only is my rock and my salvation; He is my defense; I shall not be moved. 7 In God is my salvation and my glory; The rock of my strength, And my refuge, is in God. 8 Trust in Him at all times, you people; Pour out your heart before Him; God is a refuge for us.

Deuteronomy 31:8

"And the LORD, He is the One who goes before you. He will be with you, He will not leave you nor forsake you; do not fear nor be dismayed."

DAY 26 – SETTING BOUNDARIES

Precious child and most adorned and beautiful daughter of Mine—

Within My Holy Scriptures, I have given you the directions to live a godly life. The boundaries that define who you are—where you begin, and others end—and the way in which you are to be treated are set out most clearly. I expect nothing but the utmost respect for you and for you to be cherished, for you are My forgiven and treasured daughter. The boundaries are defined by your obedience to Me and within this, your willingness to obey and to step into the Plan that I have for your life.

For you cannot serve and obey Me and be without boundaries and without clear distinctions between yourself and others. You cannot define yourself through your identity in Me and be without respect and dignity. Who you are within Me allows you to bloom and flourish. You are My chosen and cherished daughter. For I chose you and I drew you to Me, before the beginning of time. I earmarked you and I set out Whose you are and Whose I called you to be.

See this with clarity, allow it to soak into you and this then becomes your boundary and the mechanism by which you command respect. Know who you are within Me, My cherished child, and the boundaries between yourself and others will follow and fall naturally into place.

> *Galatians 2:20*
> "I have been crucified with Christ; it is no longer I who live, but Christ lives in me; and the life which I now live in the flesh I live by faith in the Son of God, who loved me and gave Himself for me."

MEREDITH SWIFT

2 Corinthians 5:17

Therefore, if anyone is in Christ, he is a new creation; old things have passed away; behold, all things have become new.

Ephesians 4:24

and that you put on the new man which was created according to God, in true righteousness and holiness.

DAY 27 – DISSOLVING BARRIERS

Precious daughter—

Allow your regrets over your marriage and the depths of your sorrow lead to your repentance over its demise. What were your actions and your thought life at that time can all be repented of and this repentance leads to a dissolving of the barriers between us. You will be drawn closer to Me as your repentance will bring down those walls of separation caused by ungodly behaviours. You will be drawn closer to Me as your repentance will give you clarity for your future actions and will produce good fruit in the days to come.

Your part in your marriage was not as an equal to your husband, nor as a true helper, and neither of you was focused truly on Me. Often your frozenness in fear caused inaction. Repent for all of this and all that was, precious child, and know that all was necessary for your growth and My glory.

Your pain served a good purpose—to build your trust in Me and for you to be an overcomer in Me, with My strength for your weakness and My love for your fear.

So shed your tears of repentance, My cherished daughter, and allow yourself to be filled with My living water, allow the whisperings of My Holy Spirit to bring you comfort unparalleled and a real hope for your future.

Lay down your burden of grief and rest now for a while.

Peace be with you.

Joel 2:12

"Now, therefore," says the LORD, "Turn to Me with all your heart, With fasting, with weeping, and with mourning." 13 So rend your heart, and not your garments; Return to the LORD your God, For He is gracious and merciful, Slow to anger, and of great kindness; And He relents from doing harm.

2 Corinthians 7:9

Now I rejoice, not that you were made sorry, but that your sorrow led to repentance. For you were made sorry in a godly manner, that you might suffer loss from us in nothing. 10 For godly sorrow produces repentance leading to salvation, not to be regretted; but the sorrow of the world produces death. 11 For observe this very thing, that you sorrowed in a godly manner: What diligence it produced in you, what clearing of yourselves, what indignation, what fear, what vehement desire, what zeal, what vindication! In all things you proved yourselves to be clear in this manner.

DAY 28 – VENGEANCE IS MINE

Cherished child—

Your thoughts of revenge and hate are as a vacuum which can never be filled; they are as a relentless and aggressive onslaught of an infection which can never be healed, yet can only became deeper and more festering, producing further sickness and pain without end or resolution.

Those past desires for revenge were not an antidote to your feelings of powerlessness but rather they were a means whereby you became even more crippled and anguished as your entrapment became more pronounced. These feelings fuelled an ungodly intention of which no good could ever come.

But know this, precious child - vengeance is Mine and I will judge every one of My human creations as they stand before Me at that judgement time, at that judgement seat. Each one will give an account for their actions. As will you, precious child. And the account will be how did you glorify Me? Did you step into the Plan I have for your life, the good and glorious plan that sees you grow and bloom with a sweet and pervading fragrance of influence to those around you as you point them towards Me? Or not?

For vengeance and thoughts of hate will surely kill all that is pure and lovely and good; like weeds if allowed to grow unchecked and without restraint, that will strangle without discrimination the flowers that stand side by side with them.

Clean up your thought life, My sweet and cherished daughter, and know that you can give that burden of revenge to Me—for I am perfectly equipped to take it from you. For it weighs you down unnecessarily.

You may believe for a time it is producing resolution within you, but it is a road which ultimately leads to a place that is not of Me. Step off the road that leads nowhere and turn back towards Me—towards My goodness, My mercy and My unfailing love for you. For I am completely trustworthy, and My words speak life into your being.

I love you and I protect you with a fierce and unmatched fire whose flames do not die. For in Me you find life everlasting.

I am your God.

Rest in Me.

Deuteronomy 32:35
Vengeance is Mine, and recompense; Their foot shall slip in due time; For the day of their calamity is at hand, And the things to come hasten upon them.

Romans 8:33
Who shall bring a charge against God's elect? It is God who justifies. 34 Who is he who condemns? It is Christ who died, and furthermore is also risen, who is even at the right hand of God, who also makes intercession for us. 34 Who shall separate us from the love of Christ? Shall tribulation, or distress, or persecution, or famine, or nakedness, or peril, or sword. 36 As it is written: "For Your sake we are killed all day long; We are accounted as sheep for the slaughter. 37 Yet in all these things we are more than conquerors through Him who loved us. 38 For I am persuaded that neither death nor life, nor angels nor principalities nor powers, nor things present nor things to come, 39 nor height nor depth, nor any other created thing, shall be able to separate us from the love of God which is in Christ Jesus our Lord.

HEART FOR WOMEN

1 Peter 3:8

Finally, all of you be of one mind, having compassion for one another; love as brothers, be tender-hearted, be courteous; 9 not returning evil for evil or reviling for reviling, but on the contrary blessing, knowing that you were called to this, that you may inherit a blessing.

1 Thessalonians 5:15

See that no one renders evil for evil to anyone, but always pursue what is good both for yourselves and for all. 16 Rejoice always, 17 pray without ceasing, 18 in everything give thanks; for this is the will of God in Christ Jesus for you.

DAY 29 – LOOSEN YOUR VOICE

Beloved woman—

You who have been chosen and are cherished more than you can ever imagine—it is time now for your voice to come back again. For so long, it was as though your voice was stifled and strangled within you, for you were in many ways forbidden to speak and to be heard. Your counsel and your freedom of speech were taken from you. This God given element of who I created woman to be is necessary to return now in order for you to bloom and flourish once again.

Read about and soak within the promises of who I have created you to be. You are so loved! In all of who you are, every part of you. That which was hidden can now be revealed again in safety and security, trusting in the God who created you and set you free, who chose you before the beginning of time and who never leaves you nor forsakes you. As you hear My voice, ask Me to loosen *your* voice once more. For your freedom to express yourself is one of the ways in which you may reclaim your identity within Me.

You are valued, precious child, more than you can possibly know or understand. There is no longer any need for the lies of the enemy to speak into your mind, nor to take away your voice. For the spirit of fear was never of Me and your trust in Me will be your protection against it having any further power over your mind, your heart and all you are.

Commit moment by moment to believing in My promises for your life - I turn evil for good, and I love you unfailingly and with a richness and beauty which are unparalleled. Nothing can separate you from My love, My cherished creation; My beloved daughter.

HEART FOR WOMEN

Let your voice be heard now.

Peace be with you.

Colossians 4:6
Let your speech always be with grace, seasoned with salt, that you may know how you ought to answer each one.

Psalm 19:14
Let the words of my mouth and the meditation of my heart be acceptable in Your sight, O LORD, my strength and my Redeemer.

Isaiah 54:17
"No weapon formed against you shall prosper, And every tongue which rises against you in judgment You shall condemn. This is the heritage of the servants of the LORD, And their righteousness is from Me," Says the LORD.

Psalm 35:28
And my tongue shall speak of Your righteousness And of your praise all the day long.

DAY 30 – RETURN TO ME

Beloved child of Mine—

You are My small, defenceless and forlorn little sheep, once separated from My flock and My loving Shepherd protection, but now returned to Me. For I came in search of you and brought you back into My loving embrace and My eternal care. I guide you, I care for you, I minister to you, I tend to your wounds, I renew your mind and hold your heart within Me. I protect you fiercely, lifting you tenderly to hold you safely within the embrace of My loving Shepherd's arms. You are a part of My body now, cherished daughter of Mine, and I will not leave you nor forsake you.

Your weakness, My precious little sheep, is made strong within Me. For the enemy may prowl like a roaring lion but he is no match for Me. My might and My power has melted mountains, has spoken all of creation into being. Every knee shall bow to Me. I am well equipped to care for you and to love you all the days of your life.

Only commit to Me and to My ways. Follow Me. Take up your Cross and follow Me. Though your road may be unknown, your destination is certain.

Peace be with you.

2 Corinthians 2:9
And He said to me, "My grace is sufficient for you, for My strength is made perfect in weakness." Therefore most gladly I will rather boast in my infirmities, that the power of Christ may rest upon me.

HEART FOR WOMEN

Isaiah 40:10

Behold, the LORD God shall come with a strong hand, And His arm shall rule for Him. Behold, His reward is with Him. And His work before Him. 11 He will feed His flock like a shepherd; He will gather the lambs with His arm, And carry them in his bosom, And gently lead those who are with young.

1 Peter 5:4

And when the Chief Shepherd appears, you will receive the crown of glory that does not fade away.

John 10:14

I am the good shepherd, and I know My sheep, and am known by My own. 15 As the Father knows Me, even so I know the Father; and I lay down My life for the sheep.

DAY 31 – CAREFUL PREPARATION

Precious daughter—

Know this—that I have a good Plan for your life. I have given you hope and a future that is of substance. Your new life begins now. Choose wisely what you fill your new life with. For just as a flower will bloom in a garden where the soil has been lovingly and carefully prepared, where it is given the right nourishment, and when there is adequate sunshine and plentiful supply of water, so too will you bloom as you grow straight and true towards Me. With careful preparation.

So, let your careful preparation now—living My way, according to My Holy Scriptures and the whisperings of My Holy Spirit to guide you in all your ways and speaking with Me in prayer and supplication—yield spectacular results in the future. Your pain and your suffering have been grievous and paralysing in their depth, yet know you have endured this for My sake and you have overcome within Me.

Your trust has been in Me and can continue to be so. I become your perfect husband and you are able to trust me completely and wholeheartedly. I do not torment, nor cripple, nor jeer at your frailties—for I, your loving Saviour who died for you—love each and every part of you. There is nothing which can be, or is, hidden from Me—for I know all about you. From the number of hairs on your head to your unique fingerprints, all has been lovingly fashioned by Me. I know every part of you and I especially know your brokenness, those parts of you which lie hidden in shadow, ashamed, afraid, weak and sorrowing beyond all measure.

And I will bring all of your brokenness together. For just as I knit you together in the womb, so too can you be knit together right here and now within Me. Your brokenness can become whole within Me. Only choose, My precious, cherished and forgiven daughter, to live My way.

This is not the easy way, yet I say to you it is the most profound way. This life is but a speck of dust, transient and fleeting, yet Eternity with Me stretches out forever and is for always. And I have prepared a place for you, My overcoming and redeemed daughter, to abide with Me.

So, walk now with confidence in Me, allow Me to guide your footsteps and know without doubt the path you now tread will be with surety and with the promise always of My unfailing love and mercy, grace and faithful care to travel with you.

Peace be with you.

John 14:1
Let not your heart be troubled; you believe in God, believe also in Me. 2 In My Father's house are many mansions; if it were not so, I would have told you. I go to prepare a place for you. 3 "And if I go and prepare a place for you, I will come again and receive you to Myself that where I am, there you may be also. 4 "And where I go you know, and the way you know."

Luke 12:7
But the very hairs of your head are all numbered. Do not fear therefore; you are of more value than many sparrows.

Psalm 68:5
A father of the fatherless, a defender of widows, is God in His holy habitation.

Colossians 2:6
As you therefore have received Christ Jesus the Lord, so walk in Him, 7

rooted and built up in Him and established in the faith, as you have been taught, abounding in it with thanksgiving. 8 Beware lest anyone cheat you through philosophy and empty deceit, according to the tradition of men, according to the basic principles of the world, and not according to Christ. 9 For in Him dwells all the fullness of the Godhead bodily; 10 and you are complete in Him, who is the head of all principality and power.

Isaiah 54:5

For your Maker is your husband, The LORD of Hosts is His name; And your Redeemer is the Holy One of Israel; He is called the God of the whole earth. 6 For the LORD has called you like a woman forsaken and grieved in spirit, like a youthful wife when you were refused," Says your God. 7 "For a mere moment I have forsaken you, But with great mercies I will gather you. 8 With a little wrath I hid My face from you for a moment; But with everlasting kindness I will have mercy on you," Says the LORD, your Redeemer.

DAY 32 – SWEET REFRESHING

Precious, redeemed one—

My peace I leave with you, My peace I give to you—and Mine is the peace which surpasses all understanding. For in Me may you truly be reconciled to God, in Me may you find the sweet and refreshing rest which permeates every part of your being, that soaks your spirit with My unending servant love. For I came to set you free, My precious child, and now I guard you jealously from harm and iniquity. Turn your face towards Me, cherished daughter, and allow your trust in Me to grow and flourish.

Realise nothing can separate us. There is no lie from the enemy that can withstand My might and power. For I, the Lord of all Creation, have chosen you and I shelter you now under the strength and fortress of My wings. Only choose My ways in each and every moment and know you are an overcomer in Me.

Though at times you may feel engulfed by your pain and the longing that things could have been different; though at times you may feel as though all has been lost, as though all is futile and without purpose, though at times you may believe you were lacking—these I promise you can be fleeting if only you will turn your face towards Me and acknowledge I am Lord of your life. Run to Me, My sweet and fragile child, and cling to Me. For I have created you for My glory and I will never leave you nor forsake you.

What you seek—the love, the peace, the mercy, the understanding, the faithfulness—is all found in Me. Yet you must be obedient to Me, you must at all times be alert to what comes into your heart and your mind—and you must guard these relentlessly. Fix your eyes on what is pure and good and lovely and fill your heart and mind with thoughts of Me. Our relationship will grow in safety and trust as I prune and cut away all that is no longer necessary for your good and My glory. In this be willing. Allow consistency and cultivate perseverance. Submit to Me, beloved daughter, and allow for this process, knowing all is well within Me. Trust in Me.

John 14:25

"These things I have spoken to you while being present with you. 26 "But the Helper, the Holy Spirit, whom the Father will send in My name, He will teach you all things, and bring to your remembrance all things that I said to you. 27 "Peace I leave with you, My peace I give to you; not as the world gives do I give to you. Let not your heart be troubled, neither let it be afraid.

Psalm 36:7

How precious is your lovingkindness, O God! Therefore the children of men put their trust under the shadow of Your wings. 8 They are abundantly satisfied with the fullness of your house, And you give them drink from the river of Your pleasures. 9 For with You is the fountain of life; In Your light we see light. 10 Oh, continue Your lovingkindness to those who know You, And Your righteousness to the upright in heart. 11 Let not the foot of pride come against me, And let not the hand of the wicked drive me away. 12 There the workers of iniquity have fallen; They have been cast down and are not able to rise.

Philippians 4:8

Finally, brethren, whatever things are true, whatever things are noble, whatever things are just, whatever things are pure, whatever things are lovely, whatever things are of good report, if there is any virtue and if there is anything praiseworthy—meditate on these things. 9 The things which you learned and received and heard and saw in Me, these do, and the God of peace will be with you.

DAY 33 – PLANTED IN MY GROUND

Precious daughter of Mine—

Now you are living My way and in My truth. Continue in this—for I have given you a new life in Me. And your new foundation is built on the rock which is Me. No more shall you be scattered to and fro like grains of sand, relentlessly pursued and tormented by guilt, shame, doubt and immobilisation through the spirit of fear—No! For now I have planted you firmly in My ground, nourished and watered by My Holy word and through My Holy Spirit.

Now with the consistency which comes from a living relationship with Me, chosen moment by moment, you can progress in trust and surety, knowing I cannot fail you. You have free will, precious daughter, so choose well. For the enemy prowls like a roaring lion and your eyes must be wide open in order to see Me. Be alert to your thought life and seek to armour yourself against the lies and the discord the enemy brings, for this is a poison to your mind. Renew your mind with My truth and with the guidance of My Holy Spirit. Take good action of Me, moment to moment, for this will be your shield and your protection.

And soak yourself in My promises, cultivate that right relationship between us as you seek Me out first and foremost in all aspects of your life. For I yearn for and delight in a relationship with you, beloved daughter, My precious creation. I am glorified by you stepping into the good Plan I have for your life and this will unfold more and more as we build relationship and I strengthen you. For your weakness is made perfect in My strength, My chosen and sanctified child. You are redeemed through My blood poured out at the Cross as I became sin for you. So, I have taken all of your suffering and you are made new now within Me.

Start afresh this moment, tender child of Mine, and put away that which has burdened you, casting all of your cares on Me, for I am mightily equipped to take these from you.

Nothing shall separate us. All is well.

John 14:6
"I am the way, the truth and the life. No one comes to the Father except through Me."

Matthew 7:24
"Therefore whoever hears these sayings of Mine, and does them, I will liken him to a wise man who built his house on the rock; 25 "and the rain descended, the floods came, and the winds blew and beat on that house; and it did not fall, for it was founded on the rock. 26 "But everyone who hears these sayings of Mine, and does not do them, will be like a foolish man who built his house on the sand; 27 and the rain descended, the floods came, and the winds blew and beat on that house; and it fell. And great was its fall."

Ephesians 6:10
Finally, my brethren, be strong in the Lord and in the power of His might. 11 Put on the whole armour of God, that you may be able to stand against the wiles of the devil. 12 For we do not wrestle against flesh and blood, but against principalities, against powers, against the rulers of the darkness of this age, against spiritual hosts of wickedness in the heavenly places. 13 Therefore take up the whole armour of God, that you may be able to withstand in the evil day, and having done all, to stand.

DAY 34 – LIFT YOUR HEAD

Sweet and fragile daughter—

Your health in all its facets is your priority at this time, precious child. So, take care of your physical body through proper rest, exercise and adequate water and nourishment; protect your mind through renewal of it and strengthening through my Scriptures; soothe your emotional state through wise counsel as well as relaxing and fun pastimes to bring balance.

Lighten your outlook as the darkness has now past and you who have been shrunken and minimised may now be able to open up and begin to bring joy into your daily life again. You cannot waste any time in this endeavour; honour Me and glorify Me by caring for your health. This is a time in your life where you are to build up who you are in Me in order to strengthen and release all I have for you. You may grow strong again whilst acknowledging there will be times when you cannot function.

Honour all of the stages of this journey, for you are grieving at this time for that which was. So, realise infinite care and gentleness are necessary as you come to terms with the toll this abuse has had on your being. At times you will surge ahead in confidence, at other times shock and fear will still threaten to paralyse you, and then again you will feel consumed with such anger that something such as this has even happened to you.

Beloved daughter, allow Me to be your strength and your comfort as all of these stages surface within you. Rest in Me. Lift your head! For you no longer have any need to hide who you are. For I have created all that is, and I am all that is and was and will be. You can come to Me, precious one, and release to Me all that has held you captive.

HEART FOR WOMEN

Only trust and know I am with you.

Peace be with you.

Romans 12:1
I beseech you therefore, brethren, by the mercies of God, that you present your bodies a living sacrifice, holy, acceptable to God, which is your reasonable service. 2 And do not be conformed to this world, but be transformed by the renewing of your mind, that you may prove what is that good and acceptable and perfect will of God.

1 Corinthians 6:19
Or do you not know that your body is the temple of the Holy Spirit, who is in you, whom you have from God, and you are not your own? 20 For you were bought at a price, therefore glorify God in your body and in your spirit, which are God's.

Psalm 3:3
But You, O LORD, are a shield for me, My glory and the One who lifts up my head. 4 I cried to the LORD with my voice, And He heard me from His holy hill. 5 I lay down and slept; I awoke, for the LORD sustained me. 6 I will not be afraid of ten thousands of people who have set themselves against me all around.

DAY 35 – LEAPING WITH JOY!

My overcoming and cherished child—

You are running swiftly precious child; you are leaping with joy! For I have delivered you out of your old life, I have saved you from the wilderness of your bondage and brought you into the lushness of new life within Me. You are filled with the living water of My Holy spirit, sent to guide you. You are an overcomer in Me, beloved daughter, and no more will you hide your face in shame but rather your face will be lifted as you stand tall.

You glory in Me, you delight in Me and I lift you high. You praise Me and honour Me with the song that is you, as you give to Me all of you in order that I may bring you into the light of a new day dawning. Submit to Me, My precious and cherished daughter, remembering I know all about you and I cannot fail you. My love is spotlessly pure and totally unimaginable in its vastness and depth. And all of this love is for you! So run, precious child, and do not grow faint at the task at hand. Moment by moment I will reveal each step to you, and you can rest in Me, knowing I lead you, yet I also walk beside you.

Ask for me to create and cultivate a clean heart within you. The old way has gone; and new life beckons you. Step into the good and glorious Plan I have for your life, truly free now from the bondage of shame that held you captive for so long.

For I love you with a fierce protectiveness, I am your shield and your salvation, and none can harm you. For I am with you, so who can be against you? None can withstand My might and My power! Only choose to stay close with Me, live My way, and within My sovereign and unending loving kindness and tender mercy.

HEART FOR WOMEN

For you are so loved, precious one. So loved!

Abide with Me.

> *Psalm 18:2*
> *I will love you, O LORD, my strength. 2 The LORD is my rock and my fortress and my deliverer; My God, my strength, in whom I will trust; My shield and the horn of my salvation, my stronghold. 3 I will call upon the LORD, who is worthy to be praised; So shall I be saved from my enemies.*

> *Luke 6:23*
> *Rejoice in that day, and leap for joy! For indeed your reward is great in heaven.*

> *Ephesians 6:16*
> *above all, taking the shield of faith with which you will be able to quench all the fiery darts of the evil one, 17 And take the helmet of salvation, and the sword of the Spirit, which is the word of God; 18 praying always with all prayer and supplication in the Spirit, being watchful to this end with all perseverance and supplication for all the saints.*

DAY 36 – TWO BECOME ONE

Beloved woman, made of man, made in My image. Good!—

Created to complement man and to be his helpmate, to nurture him, provide him with wise counsel, cleave to him and become as one. Union so strong none can divide you. You were never created, beloved one, to be dominated nor exploited, to be controlled nor made fearful. You were never created, precious daughter, to be dominated and demanded of but rather to give freely and to build up and edify your husband.

You were made in My image, cherished child, to be influenced by your husband and to be prized by him as a precious jewel, to be treasured by him and to submit to him in love and with full knowledge that while he is stronger physically, emotionally you are the one solid as a rock. For you are his safe harbour and he is your guiding light. You are complementary—each to the other—and your union is to produce good fruit and strong character within the both of you.

Neither one of you is to be less than the other—but rather to become more than; accomplishing more, much more, than either of you singly could dream was possible. A force to be reckoned with, fuelled by your focus on Me, with My precepts as your foundation and My guidance and might revealed as you work together as one. Be willing to submit to each other, in patience, kindness, gentleness and obedience to Me, the God who created you.

Rest in Me.

HEART FOR WOMEN

Ephesians 5:22

Wives, submit to your own husbands, as to the Lord. 23 For the husband is head of the wife, as also Christ is head of the church; and He is the Saviour of the body. 24 Therefore, just as the church is subject to Christ, so let the wives be to their own husbands in everything. 25 Husbands, love your wives, just as Christ also loved the church and gave Himself for her, 26 that He might sanctify and cleanse her with the washing of water by the word, 27 that He might present her to Himself a glorious church, not having spot or wrinkle or any such thing, but that she should be holy and without blemish. 28 So husbands ought to love their own wives as their own bodies; he who loves his wife loves himself. 29 For no one ever hated his own flesh, but nourishes and cherishes it, just as the Lord does the church. 30 For we are members of His body, of His flesh and of His bones. 31 "For this reason a man shall leave his father and mother and be joined to his wife, and the two shall become one flesh." 32 This is a great mystery, but I speak concerning Christ and the church. 33 Nevertheless let each one of you in particular so love his wife as himself, and let the wife see that she respects her husband.

DAY 37 – MY THOROUGH WAYS

Daughter of Courage—

Be still and know I am God. Stand! Be willing to submit to My thorough ways and allow My healing to enter into you, to flood your being with quiet surrender as My faithful and tender love soothes your troubled spirit and brings a healing balm to your fragile heart and fragmented mind. Allow Me, your Sovereign Lord and Saviour, to bring all which is shattered back into wholeness—for your heart to be clean and for you to remember you have My mind; the mind of Christ.

Offer yourself quietly before Me and allow Me to restore. For you cannot hope to do this on your own, in your singular strength. I, only I, am the God of restoration and transformation who rebuilds and begins anew within you. Yet only is this possible if you have willingness, My overcoming and cherished child. Let not your heart be troubled by how this work will occur—only be willing to be obedient to My instructions and know with certainty that you are within My good plan for your life. Glorify Me as you submit to My ways and remain open to and ready for the whisperings of My Holy Spirit at all times.

And when you can no longer stand, allow Me, your God of Ages, to cradle you in My loving embrace, lifting you up tenderly and allowing My angels to minister to you and guide you into the mystery of My glory. I bring you the peace that surpasses all understanding, that changes you so profoundly you can no longer recognise nor return to the shame that once defined you.

Only allow for this to be so.

Rest in Me.

HEART FOR WOMEN

Ezekiel 36:25
"Then I will sprinkle clean water on you, and you shall be clean; I will cleanse you from all your filthiness and from all your idols. 26 "I will give you a new heart and put a new spirit within you; I will take the heart of stone out of your flesh and give you a heart of flesh. 27 "I will put my Spirit within you and cause you to walk in My statutes, and you will keep My judgments and do them.

Psalm 139:23
Search me, O God, and know my heart; Try me, and know my anxieties; 24 And see if there is any wicked way in me, And lead me in the way everlasting.

1 Corinthians 2:9
But as it is written: "Eye has not seen, not ear heard,
Nor have entered into the heart of man
The things which God has prepared
For those who love Him.

1 Corinthians 2:16
For who has known the mind of the LORD that he may instruct Him? But we have the mind of Christ.

DAY 38 – THE MIGHT OF MY EMBRACE

Cherished child, beloved daughter of Mine—

Know this and remember it always—no battle is yours but Mine alone! For these circumstances of harshness and trying are not to be overcome through any of your fleshly machinations but rather through giving all of these to Me. For I, your all-sufficient and all-powerful God, your loving and merciful Lord and Saviour has reached down and scooped you up into the might of My embrace, keeping you safe and bolstered against all terror, all doubt, all fear, all guilt, all shame, all deception and all hollow and empty lies of the enemy.

You are not to fight in your own strength, for to do to this gives you no hope of overcoming. Rather, fix your eyes on Me, knowing that which I have already done for you through My sacrifice at the Cross has given you eternal victory in all the battles that you face.

You are to turn from the ravages of the battle you have warred in, and rather look to Me and My victory at the Cross. Glorify Me as you surrender your weapons of trying to control any part of this situation and give all to Me, your all-knowing and redeeming God. For My love for you, My sovereign power and might that have seen you redeemed and forgiven, is all-sufficient in any of the circumstances you have found—or will find—yourself within.

For this is a brand-new day. This is a fresh moment of potential. This is a tiny new seed which has been planted in the soil of My promises! You are now to tend this new and fragile seed most lovingly and carefully. Water it with My Living Water and allow the warmth of My love to be as the sunshine and nourishment that shoots forth a sprout from this seed. Continue steadfastly to care for this new seed as it takes root and grows within you straight and true until it is well established and maturing. And be vigilant to pull out the weeds of doubt and confusion as soon as they appear, so they can never overwhelm nor strangle your precious new beginning seed.

For I am doing a good work in you.

Only choose My way in willingness and in steadfast obedience.

For My love for you is unfathomable and immeasurable, gently soothing you and greatly strengthening you, all-sufficient and abounding in tender grace and sweetest of mercy.

Abide with Me!

1 Corinthians 15:57
But thanks be to God, who gives us the victory through our Lord Jesus Christ. 58 Therefore, my beloved brethren, be steadfast, immovable, always abounding in the work of the Lord, knowing that your labour is not in vain in the Lord.

Genesis 8:22
"While the earth remains, Seedtime and harvest, Cold and heat, Winter and summer, And day and night Shall not cease.

2 Chronicles 20:15
And he said, "Listen, all you of Judah and you inhabitants of Jerusalem, and you, King Jehoshaphat! Thus says the LORD to you: 'Do not be afraid nor dismayed because of this great multitude, for the battle is not yours, but God's.

DAY 39 – DAILY IMMERSION

Beloved daughter—

Prepare for growth. Open up your heart and mind to My living Word. I am both the Word made flesh and I am the Word with God. I Am.

Read My Holy Scriptures and be guided in this by the Holy Spirit. Immerse yourself daily in My Word in order to love Me with all your heart, mind, soul and strength.

This will grow our relationship. Fast for a time. Pray moment by moment. All of this will see strongholds torn down. Ask in My name for My Holy revelations.

For you have come for such a time as this.

In your weakness, I am made strong. Remember this! Celebrate this, precious child. Celebrate your deliverance not merely from the stranglehold and shackling of your past but also from the power of death, for your forgiveness at the Cross. From this, all else flows.

Be bold in your endeavours as your heart fills with Me, as your mind opens to Me, and as your Spirit comes to Me.

Remember your identity is in Me.

You are Mine, cherished and sanctified child of God.

Lay down your burden now precious child and be of good cheer.

You are an overcomer in Me and I have overcome the world!

HEART FOR WOMEN

James 5:16

"Confess your trespasses to one another, that you may be healed. The effective, fervent prayer of a righteous man avails much".

Esther 4:14

"For if you remain completely silent at this time, relief and deliverance will arise for the Jews from another place, but you and your father's house will perish. Yet who knows whether you have come to the kingdom for such a time as this?

John 1:1

In the beginning was the Word, and the Word was with God, and the Word was God. 2 He was in the beginning with God. 3 All things were made through Him, and without Him nothing was made that was made. 4 In Him was life, and the life was the light of men. 5 And the light shines in the darkness, and the darkness did not comprehend it.

John 1:14

And the Word became flesh and dwelt among us, and we beheld His glory, the glory as of the only begotten of the Father, full of grace and truth.

John 16:33

"These things I have spoken to you, that in Me you may have peace. In the world you will have tribulation; but be of good cheer, I have overcome the world."

DAY 40 – A NEW LIFE WAITING

My precious and overcoming child—

My cherished and most beloved daughter—

Know these words of communication between us will not return void, yet they will spread out and cover those who read them with the precious blanket of My overcoming and redeeming love. Know all you have gone through will be turned for good. **Know** those who read these words will recognise the presence of My Holy Spirit **which** begins the transformation process.

Know all you have gone through has built your character, precious daughter, and you may now reach out to others who have journeyed a similar path and help them to find the comfort found in Me. Help them to embrace the realisation they are not alone. Help them to believe there is a new life awaiting; that they are not defined by their circumstances but rather they can be refined through the suffering they have experienced if they allow My transforming love to fill them. Come to Me, all who are heavy laden, and I will give you rest. My yoke is easy and My burden is light.

Allow not bitterness nor regret to take root within you, My cherished possession, but allow the fruit of the spirit to flow freely and wash away all that will keep you in chains—regret, guilt, shame, unforgiveness, unbelief and hard heartedness. For I came to set the captives free. Those moments of torment are gone now and as you heal within My loving time and according to My good will and purpose you can know without doubt you are safe within Me. Your identity is within Me, immovable and unshakeable. You are well able to take up the mantle of forgiven and redeemed now.

HEART FOR WOMEN

Peace be with you My cherished and chosen daughter.

Peace be with you!

Isaiah 55:11
So shall My word be that goes forth from My mouth; It shall not return to Me void, But it shall accomplish what I please, And it shall prosper in the thing for which I sent it.

Ephesians 4:29
Let no corrupt word proceed out of your mouth, but what is good for necessary edification, that it may impart grace to the bearers. 30 And do not grieve the Holy Spirit of God, by whom you were sealed for the day of redemption. 31 Let all bitterness, wrath, anger, clamour, and evil speaking be put away from you, with all malice. 32 And be kind to one another, tender-hearted, forgiving one another, even as God in Christ forgave you.

Hebrews 12:14
Pursue peace with all people, and holiness, without which no one will see the Lord: 15 looking carefully lest anyone fall short of the grace of God; lest any root of bitterness springing up cause trouble, and by this many become defiled.

Titus 3:3
For we ourselves were also once foolish, disobedient, deceived, serving various lusts and pleasures, living in malice and envy, hateful and hating one another. 4 But when the kindness and the love of God our Saviour toward man appeared, 5 not by works of righteousness which we have done, but according to His mercy He saved us, through the washing of regeneration and renewing of the Holy Spirit, 6 whom He poured out abundantly

through Jesus Christ our Saviour, 7 that having been justified by His grace we should become heirs according to the hope of eternal life.

CONCLUSION

According to Holy Scripture, woman is created from man's rib (***Genesis 2:22***). In the physical body, the rib is the protective covering for the soft organs which are essential for the human body to function properly. So, I like to think of man as the protective covering for the softness and vulnerability of woman. Woman helps man to function properly and he covers and takes care of her. He protects her.

Protection was a key theme throughout my marriage. A big part of my despair was that I needed protection from the abusive ways of my husband. Ours was not the union described in the Bible, where a man and woman are made in God's image, created to be complementary to each other, joined together and to cleave to one another as they become one.

The role of the husband in the Bible begins with leadership and influence over his wife, which encompasses provision and protection. A husband will never be able to influence his wife if he does not care for her. He can make demands on her and she may follow as a result, but he will never truly have her heart unless he provides for her needs, cares for her wellbeing and protects her both physically and spiritually. There can be no oneness where there is manipulation, control and abuse. Rather, only separation, mistrust and division can come from these ungodly principles.

What I have learned—and continue to be uplifted and strengthened by—is how God sees me: as His precious princess and worthy of care, love and respect. I have come to realise that although God hates the divorce, our loving and merciful God does not hate the divorcee. It was my God who delivered me out of my marriage and His son Jesus who began the process of healing within me, which was only possible because of the forgiveness offered at His Holy Cross. Healing is an ongoing process and the Holy Spirit has been given to guide and minister to us. I made a choice to stay close with Jesus and healing has happened at the pace that is right for me. At times I have been impatient, but I am learning to trust in God's timing and be obedient to Him and what He is teaching me.

It took five years from when I left my ex-husband before I felt ready to divorce him. Many were the conflicting emotions and feelings on this journey of transformation—anger, shame, guilt, sorrow, revenge, sadness, love, compassion, forgiveness and joy. Many were the layers, one upon another and revealed in God's time—for instance, a layer of anger and rage would surface, which revealed the need for further forgiveness.

Forgiveness has been a crucial element in my story of freedom. Mercy has also been

vital. **Luke 6:36-37** speaks to us of a God of mercy. Over time, I chose to find it in my heart to be merciful towards my ex-husband, not to condemn him nor judge him but to reach the stage of repentance, compassion and forgiveness towards him so I could be free of the damage and trauma I had suffered at his hands.

There were times during this process when I would often feel as though I was set adrift in surging seas, swimming against a raging current—and there would be Jesus, His hand outstretched towards me, helping me to walk on water just as He helped Peter (**Matthew 14:28-32**). God met me where I was at, instilling into me His precious promises, and giving me His priceless gift of knowing who I am in Christ. And as a born-again believer in Jesus Christ, I am part of the body of Christ. All who are part of Christ—women and men—are given the right to be children of God, as well as being given the right to pray, to be forgiven, healed, delivered,

HEART FOR WOMEN

loved and ministered to by the Holy Spirit (***Galatians 3:28*** *There is neither Jew nor Greek, there is neither slave nor free, there is neither male nor female; for you are all one in Christ Jesus*).

The decision to commit to reading the Bible, God's living Word, as part of the process of learning about God and His character is also an essential part of following Jesus. Committing to reading the Bible every day has been a life changing decision for me. I truly believe seeking first the Kingdom of God does naturally ensure all else will follow. The Holy Scriptures shine light on all aspects of life and are a source of comfort and strength, especially during times of challenge. There are so many Scriptures which speak of overcoming and trusting in God when circumstances can appear to be overwhelming. Where do I begin? How can I choose? The Books of Matthew, Mark, Luke and John, the Book of Psalms and the Book of Job are some wonderful examples but there are so many more.

There are also so many Scriptures about women whom God has used mightily, and these are very comforting, inspiring and encouraging to me. Some examples are **Sarah**, whose desire for a child (***Book of Genesis***) was not fulfilled until she was 90 years of age (***Genesis 18:14*** *Is anything too hard for the Lord?*) Her son Isaac would go on to father Esau and Jacob and Jacob would father 12 sons who would become heads of the 12 tribes of Israel. David is in this bloodline, as is our Saviour Jesus; **Deborah**, a well-respected prophetess and judge whose wise decisions led to peace for Israel for 40 years (***Book of Judges***, *Chapters 4 and 5*); **Ruth and Naomi** and the sustaining mercy of God in their lives (***The Book of Ruth***); **Dorcas** (***The Book of Acts*** *Chapter 9*), a kind and charitable woman who Peter raised from the dead; Elisha the prophet and the **woman with the oil jars** (*2 Kings 4:1-7*); **Esther** in ***The Book of Esther*** – doing what must be done even though death was a very real possibility; **Hannah** and her desire for a child, who she promised she would give back to the LORD to serve Him all the days of his life (*1*

Samuel Chapters 1 and 2); **Mary**, the teenage mother of Jesus (***Matthew 1:18-25***); **Rahab**, a prostitute whose bravery and courage in sheltering the spies (***Joshua 2:1-21; 6:17-25***) led to her gaining a place in the lineage of Jesus Christ; **Jael** – who committed a murder of necessity (***Judges 4:17-24***); **Abigail**, who became King David's wife (***1 Samuel, Chapter 25***); **Mary**, the sister of **Martha**, who poured perfume over Jesus' feet (***Mark 12:1-7***); also the **woman who came to Jesus** at the home of Simon the leper and poured fragrant oil over His head (***Matthew 26:6-13***); **Priscilla** (***Acts 18:26***) with her husband Aquila, who were great teachers for Paul; the **Samaritan woman at the well** and her encounter with Jesus, resulting in her acknowledgement He was the Messiah and her powerful witness of Him (***John 4:5-42***); the **woman healed of bleeding** (***Luke 8:43-48***); the **woman about to be stoned for adultery** (***John 8:1-30***); and **Mary Magdalene** (***Luke 8:1-3; 24:10-11; John 20:1,16,18; Mark 16:9; Mark 15:40***) said to be a prostitute and renowned for her faithfulness to Christ while He was on earth.

Many of these women would almost certainly have felt dreadful paralysing fear at what they had to live out. But they did not allow the fear to stop them and God was able to work through them to accomplish His good and glorious plan for their lives.

For me, healing from the scars of domestic violence is a profoundly transforming journey and God is using this so I can help others who are where I have been. I hope with all of my heart that you, too, will commit to your journey of healing so that you, too, can step into God's wonderful plan for your life.

An even deeper hope of mine is that you have already committed yourself to walking with Jesus and having the close personal relationship He yearns for. We are created to be in relationship with God and to be saved through faith in Jesus Christ. If you have not yet made this commitment, you can begin a relationship with Jesus right here, right now and allow Him to become the Lord of your life by calling on His name and saying a simple prayer like this:

> *"Dear Lord Jesus. I ask You to come into my heart today, to live within me, to guide me and to love me and to become the Lord of my life. I know I have lived a life of sin and I am sorry for this. I turn from that life now. I acknowledge You took my sin when you died on the Cross for me. I accept Your gift of forgiveness and salvation. I want to follow You all the days of my life now. I pray this prayer in faith in the name of Jesus. Amen."*
>
> ***Romans 10:9***
> *If you declare with your mouth, "Jesus is Lord", and believe in your heart that God raised Him from the dead, you will be saved. 10 For it is with your heart that you believe and are justified, and it is with your mouth that you profess your faith and are saved.*

Welcome to the family of God! God bless you!

Now, your next step is to connect with a bible believing Church. Please contact me at http://www.meredithswift.org if you need assistance with this.

RESOURCES

DOMESTIC VIOLENCE HELP:

http://www.nationaldomesticviolencehelpline.org.uk/ (The United Kingdom)

https://www.thehotline.org (The USA)

www.dvrcv.org.au/support-services/national-services (Australia)

PRAYER MINISTRY:

Elijah House Ministries Australia – https://www.elijahhouse.com.au

Elijah House Ministries International – https://elijahhouse.org/

Elijah House Ministries have some excellent books also. I found *"Healing For A Woman's Emotions"* by Paula Sandford to be very helpful, especially the chapters on divorce and being single.

MY BOOKS

"Hearing His Voice: Meeting Jesus in the Garden of Promise – A Devotional Journey of Encouragement";

And

"From New Age To New Creation: Set Free".

ACKNOWLEDGEMENTS AND THANKS

First and foremost, I acknowledge and thank my Lord Jesus Christ for saving me and setting me free. I thank and praise Him for the wonderful life I have been given and I pray that I have glorified Him with the writing of this book.

I acknowledge and thank my wonderful launch team for their enthusiasm, excitement and support as I bring this book for publication.

I have been blessed with a loving family and a wonderful group of friends and I thank God each and every day for all of you!

A big thank you to **YOU** for reading my book! I pray that you have found it to be a blessing. I would love to connect with you! Please email me at meredith@meredithswift.org.

www.ingramcontent.com/pod-product-compliance
Lightning Source LLC
Chambersburg PA
CBHW072058290426
44110CB00014B/1732